Homes

Japanese

Cooking

Susie Donald

PERIPLUS

Ingredients

Beni shoga pink pickled ginger is eaten as an accompaniment to rice dishes, expecially sashimi.

Bonito flakes (*katsuo bushi*) readily available in plastic packs from Japanese foodstores.

Dashi a basic Japanese fish stock (for recipe, see page 4); also available in an 'instant' version whereby granules are mixed with water.

Deep-fried tofu slices (*abura-age*) must be blanched first. Pour boiling water over them, then drain well and pat dry with paper towel.

Green tea (*matcha*) powdered green tea is readily available from Japanese stores and is great for making green tea ice-cream.

Kanpyo long, thin, dried gourd strips used in sushi, in slow-cooked dishes, and to tie foods together.

Konbu dried kelp which takes the form of flat black sheets with white powder on the surface. It is used to flavour sushi rice and *dashi*.

Mirin a sweet cooking wine made from glutinous rice. Avoid products labelled '*aji-mirin*', which are a flavoured version.

Miso fermented bean paste made from soybean and a grain malt from rice, wheat or barley. Readily available.

Nori dried leaves of an ocean plant called laver, cut into squares and used for wrapping sushi and as a garnish for other dishes.

Ponzu a popular Japanese dressing made by combining 4 tablespoons lemon juice, 4 tablespoons light soy sauce, 3 tablespoons *dashi* and 1 tablespoon *mirin* and stirring well. Widely available ready-made in bottles.

Sake alcoholic beverage, commonly called Japanese rice wine.

Sesame salt (*goma shio*) this mixture of toasted black sesame seeds (either whole or ground) and salt is a popular condiment at Japanese meals.

Sesame seed sauce to make this sauce, blend together 100 g (3/4 cup) toasted white sesame seeds , 1 tablespoon *miso*, 1 tablespoon sugar, 2 tablespoons *mirin*, 2 tablespoons rice vinegar, 2 tablespoons *sake*, 6 tablespoons light soy sauce, 1 teaspoon prepared Japanese mustard and, if desired, 3 tablespoons *dashi*.

Seven-spice chilli mix (*shichimi togarashi*) a potent blend of ground chilli with other seasonings such as, mustard, *sansho*, black sesame and poppy seeds, that is often sprinkled on noodles, grilled items and one-pot dishes.

Shiitake the most commonly used mushroom in Japnese cooking is now readily available fresh or dried . It has a dark brown outer skin and a beige inner flesh and a slightly lightly woody flavour.

***Shirataki* noodles** thin strings of *konnyaku*, a glutinous paste obtained from the elephant foot plant. Eaten in sukiyaki and other hotpots, and may be replaced with mung bean vermicelli (glass or transparent noodles) if not available.

Somen very fine wheat noodles available in many colours.

Soy sauce (*shoyu*) Japanese soy sauce is readily available from Asian foodstores. The most commonly used variety is known as *koikuchi shoju*. If the recipe calls for a light soy sauce, look for *usukuchi shoju*.

Tempura dipping sauce In a bowl, combine 250 ml (1 cup) dashi, 4 tablespoons soy sauce, 3 tablespoons mirin, 3 teaspoons shredded daikon and 3 teaspoons shredded ginger and stir well to mix.

Udon these wheat noodles come in various shapes and sizes and are whiteish-beige in colour.

Wakame a kind of seaweed which must be reconstituted in water before using.

Wasabi one of the most well-known of all Japanese condiments, this very hot Japanese horseradish is sold in powdered form or as a prepared paste.

Savoury Egg Custard
(Chawan Mushi)

200 g (1 1/2 cups) bone-less chicken breast, cut in 2 1/2-cm (1-in) cubes
1 tablespoon *sake*
2 teaspoons light soy sauce
8 large prawns, peeled and deveined, tails left intact
4 large fresh *shiitake* mushrooms, stems removed, quartered
1 small carrot, peeled and thinly sliced, each slice quartered
120 g (2 cups) spinach, washed, blanched 30 seconds, drained and chopped
Zest from 1 lemon, finely grated

Dashi custard
625 ml (2 1/2 cups) *dashi*
1 tablespoon *sake*
1 teaspoon salt
4 large eggs

1 Marinate chicken in *sake* and soy for 10 minutes, then drain.
2 To prepare *dashi* custard, heat *dashi* with *sake*, soy and salt until hot and salt is dissolved. In a large bowl, combine the eggs, without beating. Stir in the *dashi* mixture in a slow, steady stream, then strain through a fine sieve.
3 Evenly divide the chicken, prawns and vegetables and arrange them in 4 small heatproof bowls. Pour egg mixture over, leaving a 2-cm (3/4-in) gap at the top of each bowl. Cover each bowl with foil or lid.
4 Heat the water in a basket steamer, and place the custards on the steamer rack; cover, with lid vented slightly so that a little steam can escape. Steam over medium–high heat for 1 minute, then reduce heat and steam gently for about 15 minutes, until a knife comes out clean, when inserted. Remove from the steamer and serve immediately, garnished with finely grated lemon zest.

Serves 4
Preparation time: **15 mins**
Cooking time: **15 mins**

Bonito Stock (Dashi)

10 cm (4 in) square piece *konbu*, wiped clean
1 litre (4 cups) water
60 ml (1/4 cup) cold water
80 g (1 cup) bonito flakes

1 Cut *konbu* into 4 equal strips. Place in a saucepan, over medium heat, with 1 litre (4 cups) water. Just before it reaches the boil, remove and discard *konbu*.
2 Add the cold water and bonito flakes. Bring to the boil, remove from heat and set aside to cool.
3 When the bonito flakes have sunk to the bottom, strain the liquid; discard the flakes. Use as required.

Yields 1 litre (4 cups)
Preparation time: **20 mins**

Sautéed Tofu

500 g (1 lb) tofu, drained
4 fresh *shiitake* mush-
  rooms, stems removed
1 medium carrot, peeled
  and shredded
1 medium potato, peeled
  and shredded
1 green capsicum (bell
  pepper), cut in julienne
  shreds
1 small leek, cut in
  julienne shreds
1 egg white
2 tablespoons light soy
  sauce
2 tablespoons *sake*
40 g (1/3 cup) cornflour

1 Cut tofu horizontally across the middle. Remove excess moisture by pressing tofu between pieces of absorbent paper.
2 Cut mushroom caps in half then slice each half finely.
3 In a medium bowl, combine the mushroom, carrot, potato, capsicum, egg white, 1 teaspoon of the soy sauce and salt to taste. Sift all but 1 tablespoon of the cornflour over the mixture and stir to mix well. Turn grill onto high.
4 Sift remaining cornflour over the tofu pieces, then pile the vegetable mixture on top. Lift tofu pieces with a spatula and place them on a griller rack. Cook under the grill for 2 to 3 minutes until vegetables are lightly cooked.

Serves 4
Preparation time: **20 mins**
Cooking time: **5 mins**

Fresh Tofu

4 *shiso* leaves
500 g (1 lb) tofu, drained
2 tablespoons light soy
sauce
2 spring onions
(scallions), finely sliced
20 g (1/4 cup) bonito
flakes
5 cm (2 in) ginger,
peeled and grated

1 Remove stems from *shiso*, make a stack with the four leaves and cut into shreds lengthways, about 3 mm thick.
2 Cut tofu into 4 equal-sized pieces and place each piece in a serving bowl.
3 Place 1/2 tablespoon soy into 4 small dishes for dipping sauce.
4 Sprinkle *shiso*, spring onion and bonito flakes over the tofu. Place a small mound of ginger on the side, and serve immediately with the dipping sauce.

Serves 4
Preparation time: **5 mins**
Assembling time: **3 mins**

Tofu with Chicken and Vegetables

4 dried Chinese black mushrooms, soaked in hot water
  for 20 minutes
300 g (10 oz) tofu
1 tablespoon vegetable oil
125 g (1 cup) lean minced chicken
2 1/2 cm (1 in) mature ginger, grated
3 tablespoons *sake*
1 medium carrot, shaved into thin wide strips
1 tablespoon sugar
2 tablespoons light soy sauce
1 egg, beaten
4 spring onions (scallions), cut in 1-cm (1/2-in) lengths

1 Drain the mushrooms and squeeze out any excess
water. Remove the stems and slice them across thinly.
2 Push tofu through a coarse sieve; leave aside to
drain.
3 Heat the oil in a medium saucepan, and sauté the
chicken for about 2 minutes, breaking it up into small
pieces with a wooden spoon.
4 Add the ginger and mushrooms and cook for a
further 2 minutes.
5 Add the *sake* and carrots over high heat and stir for
1 minute.
6 Reduce heat to medium and add the tofu, stirring
for about 1 minute until the tofu is heated through.
7 Dissolve the sugar in the soy in a small bowl and
add to the beaten egg. Add the egg mixture and stir
until just cooked, about 2 minutes. Fold through the
chopped spring onions and serve immediately.

Serves 4
Preparation time: **10 mins**
Cooking time: **10 mins**

Marinated Deep-fried Octopus

1 kg (2 lb) fresh baby
 octopus (substitute
 with squid)
120 ml (1/2 cup) *sake*
2 tablespoons soy sauce
60 g (1/2 cup) plain
 flour
Vegetable oil for deep-
 frying
4 lemon or lime wedges
 to garnish

Sauce
4 tablespoons worces-
 tershire sauce
4 tablespoons tomato
 sauce
2 tablespoons lemon
 juice

1 Clean baby octopus by peeling off the outer layer of skin under cold running water.

2 Combine the *sake* and soy in a bowl and coat the octopus in the mixture. Set aside to marinate in a cool place for 2 hours, or overnight in the refrigerator.

3 To prepare the sauce, combine the worcestershire sauce, tomato sauce and lemon juice in a small serving bowl, and set aside until required.

4 Drain the octopus, then coat each piece in flour.

5 Heat oil to 160°C (325°F), and cook 4 to 6 pieces of octopus at a time until crispy, about 2 minutes. Drain on a wire rack and repeat the process until all is the seafood is cooked.

6 Serve immediately with the sauce and lemon wedges.

Serves 4
Preparation time: **15 mins**
Cooking time: **10 mins**

Steamed Flounder
(Karei Nitsuka)

4 whole medium
flounder, about 250 g
(8 oz) each, cleaned
750 ml (3 cups) water
1 teaspoon salt
125 ml (1/2 cup) *sake*
125 ml (1/2 cup) light
soy sauce
2 tablespoons *mirin*
3 tablespoons sugar
3 cm (1 1/4 in) fresh
ginger, peeled and
shredded
125 g (2 cups) fresh
spinach, washed,
trimmed and tied in
small bundles

1 Score each fish on the upper side by making 2 parallel diagonal incisions about 3 cm (1 1/4 in) apart with a sharp knife, then making 2 further parallel incisions on the opposite diagonal. Make the cut deep enough to almost touch the bone.

2 Bring the water, salt, *sake*, soy sauce, *mirin* and sugar to the boil in a deep frying pan. Add ginger and simmer for 30 seconds.

3 Place fish in the boiling liquid in a single layer, overlapping heads and tails where necessary. When liquid returns to boiling, lower heat and simmer fish for 2 minutes.

4 Spoon liquid over fish but do not attempt to turn fish over. Cook for a further 3 minutes, continually basting with the boiling liquid, until the fish flakes easily with a fork, about 3 minutes.

5 Add spinach parcel to pan around the sides of the fish and cook for 30 seconds. Remove from heat.

6 Carefully lift fish and spinach onto serving plates, and spoon some of the cooking liquid over the top. Serve immediately with steamed rice.

Serves 4
Preparation time: 20 mins
Cooking time: 10 mins

Baked Fish with Vegetables
(Sakana Gingami Yaki)

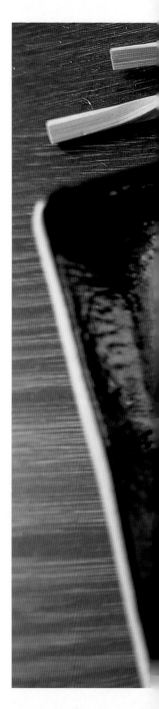

2 tablespoons *sake*
1 teaspoon light soy sauce
1 teaspoon fresh ginger juice
1 teaspoon salt
600 g (1 lb 3 oz) white fish fillets (such as flounder, sea bass and cod), cut in 4 equal pieces
4 pieces aluminium foil, 25-cm (10-in) square
1 large carrot, peeled and cut in 3 mm thickness
1 medium onion, sliced in rings, 3mm thick
1 large green capsicum (bell pepper), cut across in rings, 3 mm thick
1 tablespoon vegetable oil
1/2 medium lemon, cut into thick slices

1 Combine *sake*, soy sauce, ginger juice and salt in a shallow dish. Coat the fish well with this mixture and leave to marinate for 10 minutes. Drain, reserving marinade.
2 Heat oven to 160°C (325°F, gas 3). Place one fillet of fish on each of the squares of aluminium foil, brush with oil, then scatter the fish with carrot, onion and capsicum.
3 Sprinkle fish with remaining marinade and close the foil to make a pouch by bringing two opposite sides of the foil together and sealing over the centre of the fish. Fold up each end of the foil and place each packet on a baking tray.
4 Bake for about 20 minutes; fish should flake easily with a fork. Place foil packets on serving plate or carefully remove fish and vegetables from the foil, pouring any remaining juices over the top. Serve garnished with lemon slices.

Serves 4
Preparation time: **15 mins**
Cooking time: **20 mins**

Tempura

60 g (1/2 cup) flour for dredging

1 medium Japanese eggplant (aubergine), cut lengthways in 8 pieces

120 g (4 oz) Japanese pumpkin or sweet potato, thinly sliced

1 medium onion, cut in crescents 2 cm (3/4 in) wide

4 fresh *shiitake* mushrooms, stems removed

100 g (3 1/2 oz) green beans, tops and tails removed

90 g (2/3 cup) fresh or frozen green peas

8 large prawns, peeled and deveined with tails left intact

4 whitebait, about 60 g (2 oz) each, or white fish fillets sliced 5 mm thick

4 scallops, cleaned and sliced in half crossways

Vegetable oil for deep-frying

Tempura dipping sauce (page 3)

Batter

2 egg yolks

500 ml (2 cups) iced water

250 g (2 cups) plain flour

Serves 4
Preparation time: **20 mins**
Cooking time: **30 mins**

1 Set aside the 60 g (1/2 cup) flour in a shallow bowl with which to dredge foods to be fried.

2 Heat oil in wok or deep-fryer to 160°C (325°F). Prepare first batch of batter while the oil is heating. Lightly beat 1 egg yolk with half the iced water in a medium bowl until well mixed.

3 Add half the flour all at once, and stir briefly with a fork or chopsticks until just combined. (The batter may be lumpy but do not overmix).

4 Dredge the eggplant, pumpkin, green beans and onion pieces in flour, shaking off any excess. Dip a slice of vegetable into the batter and gently shake off any excess batter.

5 Carefully slip vegetables into the hot oil, and cook until batter is crisp and the vegetable is tender, about 3 minutes. Fry 5 to 6 pieces at a time, turning once, then remove from oil with a slotted spoon and drain on a wire rack.

6 To cook mushrooms, spoon some batter on the underside of the mushrooms, shaking off any excess batter. Place mushrooms in oil, batter-side-down, and fry until tender, about 1 minute, turning once. Remove from oil and drain.

7 Sprinkle green peas lightly with flour. Scoop about 1 tablespoon peas into a slotted spoon and coat the peas on the spoon in batter. Drain excess batter from cluster of peas via the holes in the spoon. Carefully place cluster of peas into the oil and cook for 2 to 3 minutes, turning once, until batter is crisp. Remove from oil and drain.

8 Heat oil to 180°C (350°F), and prepare second batch of batter while the oil is heating. Fry seafood pieces as before, until pale and crisp, about 3 minutes.(Prawns may take a minute more, depending on size). Remove from oil and drain on rack.

9 To serve, place a pile of shredded daikon and ginger into small sauce bowls. Pour about 3 tablespoons warm tempura dipping sauce (see page 3) into each bowl and serve with a selection of tempura.

Salmon Teriyaki
(Sake Teriyaki)

2 tablespoons light soy
1 tablespoon *mirin*
2 teaspoons *sake*
500 g (1 lb) salmon fillet, deboned, cut in four
90 g (3 oz) daikon, peeled and grated
1 tablespoon vegetable oil

1 Combine soy, *mirin* and *sake* in a small bowl and pour over salmon pieces to marinate for 10 minutes. Drain salmon, reserving marinade.
2 Heat the grill; brush griller rack lightly with oil. Place fish on rack, skin side up, and brush pieces lightly with marinade. Grill until skin is lightly browned and shrunken, about 4 minutes.
3 Turn salmon pieces and brush again lightly with the marinade. Grill until the salmon is just cooked through and the flesh flakes easily with a fork, about 4 minutes.
4 Remove fish to serving plates and spoon over a little of the remaining marinade. Serve immediately with grated daikon.

For equally delicious scallop teriyaki, substitute 500 g (1 lb) trimmed large scallops for the salmon. For grilled teriyaki vegetables, use assorted vegetables such as asparagus, eggplant, red capsicum, and shiitake mushrooms.

Serves 4
Preparation time: **15 mins**
Cooking time: **10 mins**

Grilled Skewered Chicken (Yakitori)

1 tablespoon sugar
60 ml (1/4 cup) *mirin*
125 ml (1/2 cup) light soy sauce
125 ml (1/2 cup) *sake*
500 g (1 lb) boned chicken meat, cubed
225 g (7 oz) chicken livers, cleaned and cubed
4 fresh *shiitake* mushrooms, stems removed, cut in half
2 large green capsicums (bell peppers)s, cut in 3-cm (1 1/4-in) squares
1 leek
16–20 metal or bamboo skewers, 20 cm (8 in) long
Seven-spice chilli mix

1 Combine sugar, *mirin*, soy sauce and *sake* in a medium saucepan and bring to the boil. Lower heat and allow to simmer for about 15 minutes, whilst the sauce reduces to 250 ml (1 cup).

2 If using bamboo skewers, soak in water for at least 10 minutes.

3 Thread chicken and livers onto skewers alternating with pieces of leek and capsicum.

4 Heat the grill and baste the skewers with the sauce, using a small brush.

5 Grill cook for about 30 seconds on each side, basting and turning 2 or 3 times until the chicken and livers are just cooked.

6 Serve immediately, sprinkled with seven-spice chilli mix and lemon wedges.

Serves 4
Preparation time: **30 mins**
Cooking time: **5 mins**

Deep-fried Chicken (Toriniku Tasuta-Age)

2 teaspoons fresh ginger juice
1 clove garlic, finely chopped
1 tablespoon soy sauce
1 tablespoon *sake*
500 g (1 lb) boned chicken breast, cut in 4-cm (1 1/2-in) squares
90 g (2/3 cup) cornflour
750 ml (3 cups) vegetable oil
Lemon wedges, to garnish

1 In a medium-sized mixing bowl, combine the ginger juice, garlic, soy sauce and *sake*.

2 Coat chicken pieces in marinade and let stand for 20 minutes.

3 Drain chicken and toss lightly in cornflour, shaking off any excess.

4 Heat oil to 160°C (325°F) and fry the chicken, about 4 to 5 pieces at a time, until golden and cooked through, about 4 minutes.

5 Remove with a slotted spoon and drain on a wire rack. When oil returns to 160°C (325°F) add some more chicken pieces and repeat procedure until all chicken is cooked. Keep chicken pieces warm until serving, garnished with lemon wedges.

Serves 4
Preparation time: 30 mins
Cooking time: 10 mins

Simmered Chicken Meatballs (Toriniku Dango)

500 g (1 lb) minced chicken
2 spring onions (scallions), finely chopped
3 cm (1 1/4 in) fresh ginger, peeled and grated
60 ml (1/4 cup) light soy sauce
1 medium egg
2 tablespoons cornflour
750 ml (3 cups) *dashi* (page 4)
2 tablespoons *sake*
2 tablespoons *mirin*
1 spring onion (scallion), finely sliced to garnish
Fresh coriander (cilantro) leaves to garnish

1 Combine minced chicken, spring onions, ginger, 1 tablespoon of the soy sauce and egg in a medium mixing bowl. Sprinkle in the cornflour and mix well.
2 Form chicken mixture into balls, about 3 to 4 cm (1 1/2 in) in diameter. You may need to moisten your hands with water to prevent the mixture sticking.
3 Combine *dashi, sake, mirin* and remaining soy sauce in a medium saucepan and bring to the boil.
4 Add chicken balls, one at a time, to the boiling broth, and cook for about 5 to 6 minutes. Remove balls from broth with a slotted spoon and transfer to 4 individual serving bowls. Pour on the broth and garnish with spring onion and coriander leaves.

Serves 4
Preparation time: **5 mins**
Cooking time: **15 mins**

Sesame Chicken Loaf (Matsukaze-Yaki)

- 500 g (1 lb) minced chicken
- 1 small leek, finely chopped
- 2 cm (3/4 in) fresh ginger, peeled and finely chopped
- 1 tablespoon soy sauce
- 1 tablespoon *sake*
- 1 egg, beaten
- 1 tablespoon oil
- 2 tablespoons toasted sesame seeds

1 Combine chicken, leek, ginger, soy sauce, *sake* and egg in a mixing bowl until well combined.

2 Heat oil in a 20-cm (8-in) frying pan, and spread chicken mixture evenly over the base. Cook over medium heat for 2 to 3 minutes, until underside is brown. Cut loaf into quarters, then turn the wedges over to cook the other side for a further 2 to 3 minutes.

3 Transfer to a chopping board and slice into smaller pieces for serving if desired. Sprinkle with toasted sesame seeds and serve with a green salad.

Serves 4 to 6
Preparation time: **15 mins**
Cooking time: **10 mins**

Mix chicken, leek, ginger, soy sauce, sake and egg in a bowl until well combined.

Spread chicken mixture evenly over the base of the pan and brown the underside.

Cut loaf into quarters, then turn the wedges over to cook the other side.

Slice chicken loaf into smaller serving portions on a chopping board.

Chicken with Spring Onions
(Totiniku Negi-Maki)

2 large boned chicken thighs with legs attached (about 225 g or 7 oz each)

2 cm (3/4 in) fresh ginger, peeled and finely chopped

180 ml (3/4 cup) *sake*

2 tablespoons light soy sauce

8 spring onions (scallions)

2 tablespoons cornflour

1 tablespoon vegetable oil

Serves 8
Preparation time: **40 mins**
Cooking time: **20 mins**

1 Place chicken on a working surface, skin side down, and score the flesh with a sharp knife. Press on the meat to spread it out, creating an even thickness.

2 Combine ginger, 2 tablespoons of the *sake* and the soy sauce in a medium bowl. Coat the chicken in this mixture, and leave to marinate for 20 minutes, turning occassionally.

3 Drain chicken and place skin side down on working surface. Cut spring onions to the same length as the chicken and place 3 or 4 onions across each piece of chicken. Sprinkle with an even coating of cornflour.

4 Roll each piece of chicken up and fasten with kitchen string, securing at both ends.

5 Heat oil in a 25-cm (10-in) frying pan. Add chicken rolls, seam side down, and cook gently, turning chicken frequently with tongs until evenly browned.

6 Drain fat from pan (leaving the chicken in) and add *sake*. Reduce heat to medium-low, cover and cook for 7 minutes.

7 Add reserved marinade and simmer chicken roll for 10 to 12 minutes, until tender.

8 To serve, remove string from meat and slice cross-ways in 2-cm (3/4-in) slices and spoon pan juices over the slicess.

Place 3 or 4 spring onions across each piece of chicken.

Roll up the chicken and fasten with string.

Garlic Steak
(Gyuniko Nimiku-Yaki)

2 cloves garlic
4 tablespoons light soy sauce
2 tablespoons *mirin*
4 beef fillet steaks (about 200 g or 6 1/2 oz each),
  excess fat removed
180 g (6 oz) daikon, peeled and julienned
1/2 large carrot, peeled and julienned
2 1/2 cm (1 in) mature ginger, peeled
1 tablespoon sugar
4 tablespoons vinegar
1 tablespoon vegetable oil
2 spring onions (scallions), finely sliced

1 In a small bowl combine the garlic, soy and *mirin*,
and pour it over the steaks. Leave to stand for
30 minutes, turning occasionally.
2 Dissolve sugar in vinegar and pour over the shredded
vegetables. Leave to stand for 5 minutes; then drain
and squeeze out any excess moisture.
3 Heat oil in a large frying pan over high heat. Add
the steak and sauté until done to your liking, about
3 minutes on each side for medium rare.
4 Remove steaks and place on warmed serving plates.
Sprinkle with chopped spring onion and serve with
the marinated vegetable mixture.

Serves 4
Preparation time: 30 mins
Cooking time: 10 mins

Sautéed Pork with Ginger
(Butaniku Shoga-Yaki)

3 tablespoons soy sauce
2 tablespoons fresh
  ginger juice
2 tablespoons *sake*
1 teaspoon sugar
2 tablespoons oil
500 g (1 lb) pork tender-
  loin, cut across in 3-mm
  slices
120 g (3/4 cups) Chinese
  cabbage, in 2 1/2-cm
  (1-in) squares
5 cm (2 in) mature
  ginger, peeled and cut
  in julienne shreds

1 Combine soy sauce, ginger juice, *sake* and sugar in a small bowl and stir until sugar is dissolved.
2 Heat half of the oil in a medium frying pan over high heat. Add pork and sauté until meat is half cooked, about 1 minute. Remove pork from pan and drain.
3 Add remaining tablespoon oil to the pan. Add cabbage and ginger and sauté until almost tender, about 2 minutes. Return pork to frying pan with the sauce mixture, and sauté over high heat until pork is cooked through, about 2 minutes. Serve immediately.

Serves 4
Preparation time: 10 mins
Cooking time: 6 mins

Beef and Potato Stew (Nikujaga)

4 medium potatoes,
peeled and cut into
chunks
400 g (13 oz) boneless
beef sirloin
2 medium onions
2 tablespoons oil
500 ml (2 cups) *dashi*
(page 4)
3 tablespoons *sake*
2 tablespoons sugar
3 tablespoons light soy
sauce
5 cm (2 in) mature
ginger, peeled and cut
in julienne shreds

Serves 4
Preparation time: **35 mins**
Cooking time: **20 mins**

1 Place potato chunks into a bowl of cold water.
2 Cool beef in freezer for 30 miuntes to become firm (do not freeze!) then cut across the grain into 2-mm slices, then cut each slice into 4-cm (1 3/4-in) lengths.
3 Cut onions in half lengthways, then slice each half into 3-mm slices.
4 Heat 1 tablespoon of the oil in a heavy-based saucepan over medium-high heat. Add beef and sauté until meat is just brown, about 2 minutes. Remove from pan and drain.
5 Heat remaining oil in pan over medium-high heat, then add onions and potatoes. Sauté for 2 minutes until potatoes are well coated with oil.
6 Add *dashi*, *sake* and sugar and bring to the boil over medium heat.
7 Add soy sauce and beef to pan and simmer gently until potatoes are tender, about 15 minutes.
8 Serve immediately with cooking liquid, garnished with ginger shreds.

All-in-one Hotpot
(Yosenabe)

6 mussels or large clams
250 g (8 oz) boneless
  chicken breast, cubed
250 g (8 oz) fish fillets
  (sea bass, mackerel,
  salmon), cubed
4 large scallops
180 g (6 oz) shucked
  oysters
8 large prawns, peeled
  with tail intact, deveined
8 fresh *shiitake* mush-
  rooms, stems discarded,
  tops scored crosswise
4 leaves Chinese cabbage,
  in 5-cm (2-in) squares
1 large or 2 small leeks
300 g (10 oz) tofu
1 large carrot, thinly sliced,
  blanched 1 minute
225 g (7 oz) *shirataki*
  noodles, blanched for
  2 minutes, cut in 10-cm
  (4-in) lengths
250 ml (1 cup) *ponzu*
  sauce (page 2)
6 tablespoons grated
  daikon
Pinch of cayenne pepper
1 1/2 litres (6 cups) *dashi*
  (page 4)
1 tablespoon *mirin*
1 tablespoon light soy
  sauce
1/2 teaspoon salt
1 spring onion (scallion),
  finely sliced

1 Soak mussels or clams for 5 minutes in 1 litre
(4 cups) cold water mixed with 2 tablespoons salt.
Rinse under cold running water and drain.
2 To serve, ingredients are cooked at the table in a
flameproof casserole, in about 4 batches. Take a little
of each of the chicken, fish, shellfish, vegetables,
shirataki and tofu and place in the casserole.
3 Bring the *dashi, mirin*, soy sauce and salt to the
boil, then pour enough of the boiling liquid over the
ingredients in the casserole to almost cover. Keep
remaining *dashi* mixture hot over low heat.
4 Maintaing a steady simmer, remove the items as they
cook or allow diners to serve themselves. Replenish
the casserole with remaining food items as required,
topping up with boiling *dashi* mixture if necessary.
5 To serve, pour *ponzu* sauce into small individual
dipping bowls and mix a little daikon or spring onion
into it.

Serves 4 to 6
Preparation time: 30 mins
Cooking time: 20 mins

Beef and Vegetable Hotpot
(Sukiyaki)

500 g (1 lb) beef tender-
loin, thinly sliced
250 g (8 oz) *shirataki*
noodles
250 g (8 oz) tofu, cubed
12 fresh *shiitake* mush-
rooms, stems trimmed
2 small leeks, sliced
diagonally 1 1/2 cm
(3/4 in) thick
120 g (4 oz) spinach,
washed and roughly
chopped
2 tablespoons vegetable
oil
4 eggs

Sauce
180 ml (3/4 cup) light
soy sauce
60 ml (1/4 cup) *sake*
60 ml (1/4 cup) *mirin*
125 ml (1/2 cup) water

1 Arrange prepared ingredients on a serving platter.
Break 1 egg into 4 small serving bowls.
2 Combine the sauce ingredients and set aside.
3 At the table, heat the vegetable oil in a large frying
pan. Brown about 1/3 of the beef and the leeks for
about 1 minute, then add 1/3 of the sauce. Stir in
about 1/3 each of the tofu, *shirataki*, mushrooms and
spinach, stirring continuously until foods are done to
your liking.
4 As the food cooks, diners help themselves with
chopsticks using the egg as a dipping sauce for the
hot food.
5 Cook remaining ingredients in the same manner in
two more batches.

Serves 4
Preparation time: **20 mins**
Cooking time: **20 mins**

Beef-strip One-pot
(Shabu-Shabu)

500 g (1 lb) beef tender-
loin, cut in thin strips
250 g (8 oz) *shirataki*
noodles, blanched for
1 minute, drained and
cut into 10-cm (4-in)
lengths
300 g (10 oz) tofu,
cubed
8 fresh *shiitake* mush-
rooms, stems removed
4 leaves Chinese cabbage
125 g (4 oz) spinach
leaves, washed with
stalks removed, sliced
if too large
2 medium leeks, thinly
sliced diagonally
1 quantity of sesame
seed sauce (page3)
3 spring onions
(scallions), finely sliced
1 quantity of *ponzu*
sauce (page 2)
1/2 cup grated daikon
10 cm (4 in) *konbu*,
wiped, cut in 4 equal
strips
1/2 teaspoon salt
2 cups cooked *udon*
noodles (optional)

1 Arrange beef, *shirataki*, tofu, mushrooms, cabbage,
spinach and leeks on a platter.
2 Pour sesame sauce into a small individual dish and
top with a little of the spring onion. Set aside.
3 Pour *ponzu* sauce into a small individual dish and
top with a little of the daikon. Set aside.
4 At the table, place 1 1/2 litres (6 cups) water and
konbu in a Mongolian hotpot or flameproof casserole,
and bring to the boil over medium heat. Remove and
discard *konbu* just before water boils.
5 Add about 1/4 of each of the vegetables, *shirataki*
and tofu to the hotpot. As the foods cook, diners help
themselves from the cooking pot, dipping the hot
food into the sauce of their choice. Replenish the pot
with more items as required until all food is cooked.
6 Each person cooks his own beef by holding a slice of
beef with chopsticks or a fondue fork and swishing
the beef in the simmering stock for about 20 seconds,
whilst the other items are cooking. Season with salt.
7 If serving udon noodles, cook the noodles in the
simmering broth for 3 minutes, after the other food
items have been cooked. Ladle noodles into individual
serving bowls.

Serves 4
Preparation time: 30 mins
Cooking time: 20 mins

Chicken One-pot
(Mitzutaki)

2 tablespoons rice
1 kg (2 lb) chicken, cut in 5-cm (2-in) chunks
10 cm (4 in) *konbu*, wiped clean and cut into 4 strips
1 tablespoon *sake*
1 teaspoon salt
1 teaspoon sugar
2 litres (8 cups) water
1 quantity *ponzu* sauce (page 2)
1/2 cup grated daikon
Pinch of cayenne pepper
4 leaves Chinese cabbage, cut in squares
8 fresh *shiitake* mushrooms, stems removed and tops scored
2 medium leeks, sliced diagonally
1 large carrot, peeled and thinly sliced
250 g (8 oz) *shirataki* noodles
300 g (10 oz) silken tofu, cubed
3 litres (12 cups) water
1 spring onion (scallion), finely sliced
Lime or lemon wedges
Seven-spice chilli mix or *sansho* powder
2 cups cooked udon noodles (optional)

1 Place rice in the centre of a 10-cm (4-in) square of muslin and secure with string.

2 Place rice bag, chicken, *konbu*, *sake*, salt and sugar and the 2 litres water in a large saucepan and bring to the boil over medium heat. Just before the water boils, remove and discard the *konbu*. Reduce heat and simmer, occasionally skimming the surface to remove foam, for about 20 minutes.

3 Whilst chicken is cooking, place some *ponzu* sauce in 4 small serving bowls. Mix daikon and cayenne together and place in small bowl to serve as garnish. Arrange prepared vegetables, *shirataki* and tofu on platter.

4 Remove and discard rice. from the chicken Drain, retaining the liquid, and place chicken pieces in the pot used for cooking at the table. Strain the cooking broth and pour over the chicken.

5 At the table heat the chicken and broth until boiling. Add about 1/4 of each of the items on the platter. As each kind of food is cooked, diners help themselves from the cooking pot. Add more vegetables, *shirataki* and tofu to the pot as required. Serve with seven-spice chilli mix and lime wedges to garnish.

6 If using udon noodles, add cooked noodles to pot after chicken and other items are served, and simmer for 3 minutes. Ladle into individual bowls and serve.

Serves 4
Preparation time: 30 mins
Cooking time: 40 mins

Japanese Mixed Grill
(Teppanyaki)

4 large mussels, scrubbed with beards removed

500 g (1 lb) lean boneless meat (2 or 3 types of either chicken, beef tenderloin, lamb, liver or pork), cut in 4-cm (1 3/4-in) squares of 3 mm thickness

8 jumbo prawns, peeled with tails intact

8 fresh *shiitake* mushrooms, stalks trimmed

2 large green capsicums (bell peppers), cut lengthways into eight

2 small leeks, cut across in 5-cm (2-in) lengths

2 medium brown onions, cut in wedges

1 large carrot, peeled and thinly sliced

2 ears corn, husked and cut crossways in quarters

1 large sweet potato

180 g (6 oz) Asian eggplants (aubergines), thinly sliced diagonally

Sesame seed sauce (page 3)

Ponzu sauce (page 2)

1/2 cup grated daikon

2 spring onions (scallions), finely sliced

1 tablespoon oil

4 tablespoons seven-spice chilli mix

60 ml (1/4 cup) Japanese mustard

1 Peel sweet potato and thinly slice. Soak in cold water to prevent slices turning black.

2 At the table, heat the oil in a large frying pan or griddle pan over medium heat, and add about 1/4 of each ingredient to pan. Cook until desired doneness, 4 to 6 minutes, turning occasionally. As food is cooked, diners help themselves from the pan, which is then replenished from the platter.

3 Serve with choice of sesame seed sauce, *ponzu* sauce, grated daikon, spring onion, seven-spice powder and mustard.

Serves 4 to 6
Preparation time: 5 mins
Cooking time: 15 mins

Spinach with Sesame Seed Dressing
(Horenso Goma-Ae)

3 tablespoons white sesame seeds
1/2 teaspoon sugar
2 tablespoons light soy sauce
3 tablespoons *dashi* (page 4)
Large pinch of salt
500 g (1 lb) fresh spinach, washed, thick stems discarded
1 teaspoon vegetable oil

Serves 4
Preparation time: 10 mins
Cooking time: 5 mins

1 Brown the sesame seeds in a heavy based frying pan over low heat until golden brown, about 3 minutes.
2 Set aside 1 teaspoon of the toasted sesame seeds for garnish. Using a mortar and pestle, grind the remaining seeds until smooth.
3 Blend in the sugar, soy sauce and *dashi* to make the dressing. Set aside.
4 Drain excess water from the washed spinach. Heat oil in a medium saucepan and add a handful of the spinach leaves, stirring with a wooden spoon until leaves have wilted. Continue stirring, adding more spinach as each previous batch cooks down.
5 Place cooked spinach in a colander to squeeze out any excess moisture. Combine spinach and dressing in a small bowl, and serve either hot or at room temperature. Garnish with reserved sesame seeds.

Bean Sprout and Pepper Salad
(Moyashi Sujoyu)

250 g (2 1/2 cups) bean
  sprouts, tails removed
1 large carrot, peeled and
  cut in julienne strips
1 large green capsicum
  (bell pepper), cut in
  julienne strips
2 teaspoons toasted
  sesame seeds, for
  garnish

Dressing
3 tablespoons light soy
  sauce
2 tablespoons rice vinegar
1 tablespoon vegetable oil
1 teaspoon sesame oil

1 Wash bean sprouts in cold water and drain well.
2 In a saucepan of well-salted boiling water, blanch
the carrots for 30 seconds. Add the bean sprouts and
green capsicum and cook for a further 30 seconds.
Drain and plunge vegetables into a pan of ice-cold
water. When cool, drain well in a colander; set aside.
3 Combine the dressing ingredients in a small bowl.
4 Just before serving, place the cooked vegetables
in a serving bowl. Toss the dressing through until
thoroughly mixed. Garnish with toasted sesame seeds
and serve immediately.

Serves 4
Preparation time: **20 mins**
Cooking time: **3 mins**

Wakame and Tuna with Soy Dressing
(Wakame Sujoyu-Ae)

10 g (1/3 oz) dried *wakame*
3 tablespoons rice vinegar
2 tablespoons light soy sauce
1 teaspoon sugar
2 teaspoons sesame oil
340 g (11 oz) canned water-packed tuna, well drained
2 teaspoons lemon juice
1 medium Japanese cucumber, thinly sliced
1 large tomato, diced

1 Soak the dried *wakame* in a bowl of cold water to soften, about 20 minutes. Drain, bring a small pan of water to the boil. Cook the *wakame* for 30 seconds, then drain and rinse under cold water. Dry on paper towel. Remove any hard veins from the *wakame*, then slice it into 1-cm (1/2-in) strips.

2 Combine vinegar, soy sauce, sugar and oil in a small bowl, stirring until sugar is dissolved.

3 In a medium bowl, sprinkle tuna with lemon juice and break into bite-sized pieces using a fork.

4 Combine *wakame*, cucumber, and tomato with the tuna and toss through the salad dressing. Serve immediately.

Serves 4
Preparation time: **30 mins**
Assembling time: **3 mins**

Eggplant with Miso
(Nasu Miso-Itame)

125 ml (1/2 cup) water
60 ml (1/4 cup) *miso*
2 tablespoons light soy
  sauce
2 tablespoons sugar
3 tablespoons oil
5 cm (2 in) fresh ginger,
  finely chopped
500 g (1 lb) Japanese
  eggplant (aubergine),
  cut across into chunks
1 large red or green
  capsicum (bell pepper),
  cut into chunks
2 tablespoons *sake*
2 teaspoons cornflour,
  mixed with a little
  water

1 In a small bowl, combine the water, *miso*, soy sauce and sugar, and stir until sugar is dissolved.

2 Heat oil in a wok over high heat, then add ginger, eggplant and capsicum, stirring until vegetables are almost tender, about 3 minutes.

3 Add *sake* and stir for 20 seconds then add the miso mixture.

4 Stir in cornflour until sauce thickens, and serve immediately.

Serves 4
Preparation time: **10 mins**
Cooking time: **5 mins**

Japanese Pumpkin
(Kabocha Nimono)

500 g (1 lb) Japanese
  pumpkin
500 ml (2 cups) *dashi*
  (page 4)
2 tablespoons sugar
1 tablespoon *mirin*
2 tablespoons light soy
  sauce

1 Cut pumpkin into 5-cm- (2-in-) square chunks, leaving the skin on. Using the sharp point of a knife remove small pieces of skin to give a mottled effect. Place pumpkin, skin-side-down in a heavy-based saucepan. Add 375 ml (1 1/2 cups) *dashi*, sugar and the *mirin* and place lid on top of saucepan.
4 Bring to a gentle boil and cook for about 8 minutes, turning pumpkin over halfway through.
5 Add soy sauce and remaining *dashi*.
6 Simmer covered until pumpkin is tender. Serve immediately or leave to cool to room temperature.

Serves 4
Preparation time: **10 mins**
Cooking time: **20 mins**

Clear Soup with Scallops and Asparagus
(Hotegai Sumashi Jiru)

8 large scallops, cleaned with musde removed
4 asparagus spears, thick ends trimmed, halved
Lemon zest from 1/4 lemon, shredded
500 ml (2 cups) water
1 teaspoon salt
1 litre (4 cups) *dashi* (page 4)
1 teaspoon light soy sauce

1 Place *dashi*, lemon zest and salt in a small medium saucepan and bring to the boil.
2 Add scallops and cook for 1 minute .
3 Add asparagus and soy sauce and remove from heat.
4 Place two scallops in each serving bowl and ladle the soup over the prawns, dividing the asparagus and lemon zest between the four bowls.

Serves 4
Preparation time: **10 mins**
Cooking time: **4 mins**

Vegetable Soup
(Kenchin-Jiru)

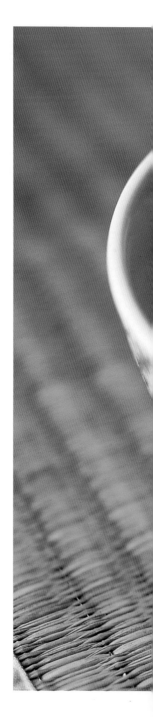

500 ml (2 cups) water
1 teaspoon vinegar
120 g (4 oz) burdock root, peeled
250 g (1 cup) tofu
1 teaspoon vegetable oil
1 teaspoon sesame oil
120 g (1 cup) minced chicken
1 medium potato, peeled, quartered, sliced thinly
120 g (4 oz) daikon, peeled, quartered, sliced thinly
1 large carrot, peeled, quartered, sliced thinly
1 1/4 litres (5 cups) *dashi* (page 4)
1 tablespoon soy sauce
1 teaspoon salt
4 *shiitake* mushrooms
4 spring onions (scallions)
Seven-spice chili mix or *sancho* powder

1 Mix half the water with the vinegar in a medium bowl. Shave the burdock root into long, thin shavings and soak in vinegared water for 5 minutes. Rinse and drain before using.
2 Using a fork break the tofu roughly into pieces about 1 1/2 cm (3/4 in) square.
3 Heat both oils in a medium saucepan, and when hot, add the chicken. Sauté, chicken, stirring constantly until just cooked, about 1 minute.
4 Add burdock root, potato, daikon and carrot, and cook, stirring constantly for another 2 minutes.
5 Add *dashi*, soy sauce and salt and heat until boiling. Lower the heat and simmer until vegetables are tender, about 4 minutes.
6 Stir mushrooms and tofu into soup, and cook for 2 minutes. Add spring onions and remove from heat.
7 Serve immediately with the seven-spice or *sancho* powders.

Serves 4
Preparation time: **20 mins**
Cooking time: **12 mins**

Tofu and Bamboo Shoot Soup
(Tofu Takenoko Miso-Shiru)

180 g (6 oz) tofu, cubed
100 g (1 cup) bamboo
shoots, cut in shreds
1 litre (4 cups) *dashi*
(page 4)
3 tablespoons *miso*

1 Place *dashi* and bamboo in a medium saucepan and bring to the boil.
2 Boil for 1 minute, then add the tofu.
3 Place miso in large ladle and dissolve it with some of the hot soup, stirring it with a wooden spoon. Stir the miso into the saucepan, then add the soy sauce.
4 Reheat soup, and when boiling, ladle it into 4 serving bowls. Serve immediately.

Serves 4
Preparation time: **5 mins**
Cooking time: **5 mins**

Egg Drop Soup
(Kakitama-Jiru)

100 g (3 1/2 oz) bone-
less, skinned chicken
breast, cut in 2 x 4-cm
(3/4 x 1 1/2-in) strips
1 tablespoon *sake*
1/2 teaspoon salt
1 litre (4 cups) *dashi*
(page 4)
1 teaspoon light soy
2 eggs, beaten
180 ml (3/4 cup) water
8 thin, decorative slices
carrot, blanched, for
garnish

1 Mix chicken strips in a small bowl and with *sake* and
1/4 teaspoon salt. Marinate for 5 to 10 minutes.
2 Heat *dashi* in a medium saucepan until boiling.
3 Add 1/4 teaspoon salt, soy sauce and chicken to the
dashi and cook for 1 minute.
4 Slowly pour 1/3 beaten egg into the soup whilst
stirring constantly. When soup returns to the boil, add
another 1/3 of the mixture, stirring constantly. Bring
soup back to the boil, add the final amount of egg
and, when all the egg 'threads' are formed, remove
from the heat.
5 Ladle soup into 4 serving bowls and garnish with
carrot. Serve immediately.

Serves 4
Preparation time: **20 mins**
Cooking time: **15 mins**

Plain Steamed Rice
(Gohan)

660g/ 3 cups medium grain rice
750ml/ 3 cups water

Serves 4-6
Preparation time: 5 mins
Cooking time: 35 mins

1 Cover rice in cold water and wash it thoroughly by rubbing between your hands until the water is quite cloudy. Drain and repeat this process several times until the water rises off clear.

2 Place the rice in a heavy-based saucepan with the water, cover with a lid, and bring to the boil.

3 Once boiling, lower the heat and simmer for 20 minutes. By this time most of the water will have been absorbed. Remove from the heat and leave rice to stand for a further 10 minutes with the lid on.

4 Using a wet rice paddle or a fork, fluff up the rice and serve in heated individual rice bowls.

Rice with Three Toppings
(Sanshoku-Gohan)

400 g (2 cups) short-grain rice
2 tablespoons sugar
2 tablespoons light soy sauce
2 tablespoons *sake*
250 g (1 3/4 cups) minced chicken
300 g (2 cups) fresh peas
8 eggs, lightly beaten1 tablespoon ginger juice
1/2 teaspoon salt
Shredded *beni shoga*, to garnish

Serves 4
Preparation time: 15 mins
Cooking time: 30 mins

1 Cook rice as in recipe for *gohan*, following steps 1 through 4, but keep rice warm in covered saucepan until required.

2 Dissolve half the sugar in half the soy sauce, half the *sake*, and the ginger juice in a medium saucepan. Bring to the boil and add chicken stirring with a wooden spoon to break up the pieces of chicken until cooked through, about 3 minutes. Remove from heat and set aside.

3 Cook peas in boiling water until tender, about 4 minutes. Drain and set aside.

4 Place eggs, salt and remaining *sake*, soy sauce and sugar in a medium saucepan. Cook over low heat, stirring constantly until eggs are set but still moist, about 4 minutes. Remove from heat.

5 Divide rice among 4 individual bowls and place equal amounts of the three topping over the rice in clear sections. Garnish with *beni shoga* and serve immediately.

Pink Rice with Beans
(Sekihan)

140 g (3/4 cup) azuki (red beans), washed and drained
750 g (3 1/2 cups) *mochigome* (glutinous rice), washed and drained

Sesame salt (*goma shio*)
1 tablespoon black sesame seeds
2 teaspoons salt

1 Place the azuki in a medium saucepan and cover with water. Bring to the boil then drain, cover with fresh cold water and bring to the boil again.

2 Reduce the heat, cover with a lid and gently simmer until beans are tender, about 40 minutes, adding more water from time to time to keep beans covered. Drain, keeping the reserved liquid.

3 Pour the liquid from the azuki onto the rice and leave covered to stand overnight to allow the rice to take on a pinkish colour.

4 Make the sesame salt by dry-roasting the sesame seeds in a frying pan until they start to leap in the pan. Transfer to a bowl and coat in the salt. Leave to cool and use as required.

5 Drain the rice and reserve the liquid. Combine the beans and rice, taking care not to crush the beans. Bring fresh water to the boil in the base of a steamer. Line the steamer with muslin or a banana leaf and spread the rice and beans mixture over. Make a few holes in the rice for the steam to escape.

6 Steam over high heat until the rice is cooked, about 50 minutes, basting frequently with the reserved azuki liquid.

7 Serve in individual heated serving bowls and sprinkle sesame salt over the top. This dish can also be served at room temperature.

Serves 4 to 6
Preparation time: **5 mins + overnight soaking**
Cooking time: **35 mins**

Deep-fried Tofu Noodles
(Kitsune Udon)

4 pieces deep-fried tofu
  slices (*abura-age*),
  about 200 g (6 1/2 oz)
2 litres (8 cups) water
400 g (13 oz) dried *udon*
  noodles
1 1/2 litres (6 cups)
  dashi (page 4)
2 tablespoons sugar
100 ml (3/4 cup +
  2 tablespoons) light
  soy sauce
3 tablespoons *mirin*
1/2 teaspoon salt
1 medium leek, washed
  and thinly sliced
Seven-spice chilli mix

1 Blanch tofu by placing it in a sieve and pouring boiling water over it. Drain and pat dry with paper towel. Cut each piece of tofu into quarters to yield 16 pieces.

2 Bring the water to the boil and add the noodles, stirring gently to keep them separate. Cook at a full, rolling boil for 5 minutes, until tender but firm. Drain and rinse under cold, running water. Drain again and cover with a damp kitchen towel.

3 Place 250 ml (1 cup) *dashi* with the sugar and tofu in a saucepan and bring to the boil. Reduce heat and cook gently for 2 minutes, then add 2 tablespoons of the soy and simmer until almost all the liquid has absorbed. Remove from heat.

4 Heat remaining *dashi*, soy sauce, *mirin* and salt over high heat. When boiling, add leek and remove from heat.

5 Warm noodles if necessary by immersing them briefly in boiling water; drain and divide into 4 individual serving bowls. Top with tofu and ladle broth over the tofu, making sure each bowl has some of the leek. Serve immediately with the seven-spice chilli mix.

Serves 4
Preparation time: **10 mins**
Cooking time: **20 mins**

Cold Soba Noodles (Zaru-Soba)

2 litres (8 cups) water
300 g (10 oz) dried *soba* noodles
350 ml (1 1/3 cups) *dashi* (page 4)
5 tablespoons light soy sauce
3 tablespoons *mirin*
1 tablespoon sugar
1 sheet toasted *nori*, cut in fine strips with scissors
2 spring onions (scallions), finely sliced
4 teaspoons *wasabi* powder mixed with enough warm water to make a firm paste

1 Bring the water to a boil in a large saucepan over high heat and add noodles, stirring gently to keep them separate. Cook noodles at a full rolling boil until firm but tender, about 5 minutes. Drain in colander and rinse under cold running water. Drain again and cover with a damp kitchen towel until completely cooled.
2 Heat *dashi*, soy, *mirin* and sugar in a small saucepan, until sugar is dissolved. Cool completely and keep aside for later use.
3 Divide cold noodles between four individual serving bowls and top each bowl with 1/4 of the *nori*.
4 Pour dipping sauce into 4 small bowls and mix some *wasabi* and spring onion into each. Diners should dip the noodles into the sauce before eating.

Serves 4
Preparation time: **10 mins**
Cooking time: **15 mins**

Chilled Noodles (Hyashi-Somen)

375 ml (1 1/2 cups) *dashi*
90 ml (1/3 cup) *mirin*
90 ml (1/3 cup) light soy
   sauce
400 g (13 oz) *somen*
   noodles
12 large tiger prawns,
   peeled and deveined,
   with tails intact
Iced water + 12 ice cubes
2 medium ripe tomatoes,
   each cut into 6 wedges
1 Japanese cucumber,
   thinly sliced diagonally
2 spring onions
   (scallions), finely sliced
2 tablespoons freshly
   grated ginger

Serves 4
Preparation time: **30 mins**
Cooking time: **5 mins**

1 Make a dipping sauce by heating together the *dashi*, *mirin* and soy until boiling. Set aside until cool.

2 In a large saucepan, bring 2 litres (8 cups) water to the boil then add noodles stirring gently to keep them separate. Cook noodles at a full rolling boil until firm but tender, about 4 minutes. Drain in a colander and rinse in cold running water. Drain again and cover with a damp kitchen towel until completely cooled.

3 Bring 500 ml (2 cups) salted water to the boil, and poach prawns until they turn pink and opaque, about 1 minute. Drain and cool.

4 Divide noodles between 4 serving bowls and add iced water until the water is level with the top of the noodles. Add 3 ice cubes to each bowl then arrange the prawns, tomato and cucumber on top.

5 Place spring onions and ginger in separate small dishes and pour dipping sauce into four small bowls. Mix the garnishes into the dipping sauce according to taste before dipping the noodles, prawns and vegetables into the dipping sauce.

Japanese Sponge Cake
(Kasutera)

5 eggs
150 g (2/3 cup) caster (superfine) sugar
60 ml (1/4 cup) honey
3/4 teaspoon baking powder
90 g (3/4 cups) plain (all-purpose) flour
Icing (confectioners') sugar for dusting
23-cm- (9-in-) square cake tin, greased and floured

1 Preheat oven to 350°F (180°C, gas 4).

2 In a medium bowl, beat the eggs until frothy, then gradually beat in the sugar and honey. Continue beating until the mixture is thick and pale and the beaters leave a ribbon trail, about 12 minutes.

3 Sift the baking powder and flour together, then sift them into the bowl.

4 Gently fold the dry ingredients into the egg mixture until just combined, then carefully pour the mixture into the prepared cake tin.

5 Bake for 30 minutes, then transfer to a wire rack and leave to cool completely.

6 Dust with icing sugar and cut into squares before serving.

Serves 6 to 8
Preparation time: 10 mins
Cooking time: 30 mins

Beat the egg mixture for about 12 minutes until it leaves a ribbon trail.

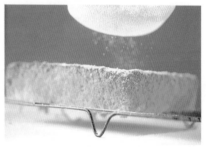

Cool the cake on a wire rack and dust with icing sugar.

Green Tea Ice-cream

600 ml (1 lb 5 oz) vanilla
ice-cream
1 tablespoon *matcha*
(powdered green tea)
400 g (13 oz) can sweet-
ened azuki beans
(optional)

Blend the ice-cream and *matcha* together then freeze
until required. For an interesting variation, serve
green tea ice-cream with sweetened azuki beans.

Serves 4
Preparation time: **5 mins**

Peach Jelly (Momo No Kanten)

1 long block *kanten*
  (agar-agar)
500 ml (2 cups) water
330 g (1 1/2 cups) sugar
1/2 cup fresh white
  peach pulp (from about
  2 small peaches)
Juice of 1/2 lemon
2 egg whites

1 Rinse the *kanten* in cold water, then cover with the water and leave to soak for 20 to 30 minutes.
2 Gently bring to the boil until dissolved, then stir in the sugar until completely dissolved.
3 Fold in the peach pulp with the lemon juice and set aside until completely cooled.
4 Beat the egg whites until stiff, then fold in the cooled mixture.
5 Pour into a shallow dish and chill in the refrigerator until set. Cut into small squares and serve.

Serves 4
Preparation time: **50 mins**
Cooking time: **20 mins**

Index

Desserts

Green Tea Ice-cream 62

Japanese Sponge
Cake 60

Kasutera 60

Momo No Kanten 63

Peach Jelly 63

Fish & Seafood

Baked Fish with
Vegetables 14

Marinated Deep-fried
Octopus 11

Karei Nitsuka 13

Sakana Gingami Yaki 14

Sake Teriyaki 18

Salmon Teriyaki 18

Steamed Flounder 13

Tempura 17

Meat & Poultry

Beef and Potato Stew 31

Butaniku Shoga-Yaki 30

Chicken with Spring
Onions 27

Deep-fried Chicken 21

Garlic Steak 28

Grilled Skewered
Chicken 20

Gyuniko Nimiku-Yaki 28

Matsukaze-Yaki 24

Nikujaga 31

Sautéed Pork with
Ginger 30

Sesame Chicken Loaf 24

Simmered Chicken
Meatballs 22

Toriniku Dango 22

Toriniku Tasuta-Age 21

Totiniku Negi-Maki 27

Yakitori 20

One-pot Dishes

All-in-one Hotpot 32

Beef and Vegetable
Hotpot 35

Beef-strip One-pot 36

Chicken One-pot 38

Japanese Mixed Grill 40

Mitzutaki 38

Shabu-Shabu 36

Sukiyaki 35

Teppanyaki 40

Yosenabe 32

Rice & Noodles

Chilled Noodles 59

Cold Soba Noodles 58

Deep-fried Tofu
Noodles 56

Gohan 52

Hyashi-Somen 59

Kitsune Udon 56

Pink Rice with Beans 55

Plain Steamed Rice 52

Rice with Three
Toppings 52

Sanshoku-Gohan 52

Sekihan 55

Zaru-Soba 58

Soup

Clear Soup with Scallops
and Asparagus 47

Egg Drop Soup 51

Hotegai Sumashi Jiru 47

Kakitama-Jiru 51

Kenchin-Jiru 48

Tofu and Bamboo Shoot
Soup 50

*Tofu Takenoko Miso-
Shiru* 50

Vegetable Soup 48

Tofu

Chawan Mushi 4

Fresh Tofu 7

Sautéed Tofu 6

Savoury Egg Custard 4

Tofu with Chicken and
Vegetables 9

Vegetables

Bean Sprout and Pepper
Salad 43

Eggplant with Miso 45

Horenso Goma-Ae 42

Japanese Pumpkin 46

Kabocha Nimono 46

Moyashi Sujoyu 43

Nasu Miso-Itame 45

Spinach with Sesame Seed
Dressing 42

Wakame and Tuna with
Soy Dressing 44

Wakame Sujoyu-Ae 44